D1307711

THE FARM

SEASONS ON THE FARM

Ann Larkin Hansen

ABDO & Daughters

Published by Abdo & Daughters, 4940 Viking Drive, Suite 622, Edina, Minnesota 55435.

Printed in the United States.

Cover Photo credits: Peter Arnold, Inc.
Interior Photo credits: Peter Arnold, Inc.

Edited by Julie Berg

Library of Congress Cataloging-in-Publication Data

Hansen, Ann Larkin.
Seasons on the farm / Ann Larkin Hansen.
p. cm. -- (The farm)
Includes index.
Summary: Describes how each season of the year affects farmers and the work they do.
ISBN 1-56239-624-2
1. Farm life--Juvenile literature-- 2. Farms----Juvenile literature. 3. Seasons--Juvenile literature. [1. Farm life. 2. Farms. 3. Seasons.] I. Title. II. Series: Hansen, Ann Larkin. Farm.
S519.H378 1996 96-11090
630--dc20 CIP
AC

About the author

Ann Larkin Hansen has a degree in history from the University of St. Thomas in St. Paul, Minnesota. She currently lives with her husband and three boys on a farm in northern Wisconsin, where they raise beef cattle, chickens, and assorted other animals.

Contents

The Rhythm of Farming

All farm work has to be done at the right time and in the proper season. The first thing every farmer does in the morning is to look outside and see what the weather is like.

If it is springtime and sunny, the farmer must begin **plowing**. If it is summer and rainy, cutting the hay must wait. If there has been a hard frost in autumn, there may be no time left to **harvest** crops. On a farm, seasons are more important than clocks.

Opposite page: Cotton harvest season in Arizona.

Getting Ready

Farmers get restless in the early spring. They know there is plenty of work ahead. They are anxious to get started. **Seed** and **fertilizer** are piled in the shed. But the seed can't be planted into cold, wet **soil** or it will **rot**.

While they wait for the warm-up, farmers tend to other **chores**. Fences are mended or built. All machinery is greased and oiled. Fruit growers **prune** their trees and bushes. **Dairy** farmers spread the winter's **manure**.

Opposite page: A farmer shoes his horse.

Hurry Up and Wait

The farmers have been hurrying to get their farms ready for spring. Now they wait. Each day, they walk their fields. They pick up clods of dirt and squeeze them in their hands. If they turn into sticky balls, the **soil** is too wet. If the dirt falls into damp, sweet crumbs, it is time to plant.

All over the world, **plows** and **planters** are hitched to tractors and oxen. Farmers plow all day and sometimes into the night. There is no time to waste. If the crop is planted too late, it won't have enough time to ripen.

Opposite page:
A farmer in Bangladesh plowing a field with a team of oxen.

Start-up

Once spring arrives, everyone is busy. Farmers no longer have time to visit with friends and neighbors. **Seed** dealers, machinery repair shops, and **fertilizer** salesmen try to keep up. As spring moves north, rice, cotton, vegetables, corn, soybeans, wheat, and potatoes are planted.

Farmers eat lunch in the fields. There is no time to stop. After planting, it is time for the first cutting of hay. Sheep are **lambing** and beef cows are **calving**. Many farmers don't get much sleep in the spring!

Opposite page:
A farmer planting sugarcane in Florida.

Summer Jobs

Finally, the crops are in. But for many farmers there is no time to slow down. All the new lambs and calves must be **wormed** and **vaccinated**. Fruit crops must be **sprayed** for bugs. Weeds in the fields must be killed with sprays or **cultivators**.

On farms with cattle, sheep, or horses, making hay is the most important summer job. In the Midwest, hay may be cut four or more times in a summer. In many parts of the West, there is only enough rain to grow one crop of hay.

Opposite page:
Hay bales in the field.

Project Time

About midsummer there is finally time to slow down. The hay is cut and won't be ready again for a month. The corn is high enough to shade the weeds. There is time for working around the buildings and shop.

Barns and sheds get new roofs. Farm houses are painted. There is time to trim the weeds in the yard, or finish a new shed for calves. If a farmer is lucky, there is even time to go fishing!

Opposite page: Loading hay into the barn is a big project.

Fairs, Shows, and Auctions

Late summer is the time for county fairs. The best farm animals, the best fruits and vegetables, and the best field crops are displayed. Farm families often spend several days at the fair with their animals, only going home to do **chores**.

Summer also is the time of rodeos, cattle shows, and farm equipment shows. Farmers go to **field days** at other farms to see what is new. Many **auctions** are held in the summer, where all sorts of equipment and animals are sold.

A farm girl is preparing her calves for judging at the State Fair.

The Busiest Time of All

The first cool weather means the busiest time of year for farmers: **harvest** time. Most crops must be harvested before winter. The weather must be dry and the **soil** firm. As soon as conditions are right, the big **combines** begin moving through the fields day and night.

Apples are picked, sorted, and sold. Vegetables are packed into boxes and shipped in refrigerated trucks. Sugar beets are rushed to the sugar factory. Wheat, soybeans, and corn must be combined and dried.

Baskets of harvested tomatoes in New Jersey.

Fall on the farm.

Getting Ready for Winter

As the days get shorter and the weather becomes cooler, **harvest** begins to wind down. When a farmer is done with a machine for the year, it is cleaned, greased, and put away. Young cattle and sheep are sent to **market**. And corn is stored in bins.

The farm gets quieter. The fields are empty now, and the fruit trees lose their leaves. Farmers with **woodlots** chop firewood for the winter. Water lines are **insulated** so they won't freeze in cold weather.

Opposite page: A corn bin filled with corn.

Time for Resting and Paperwork

By early winter, the **harvest** is gathered and sold. Animals are settled in winter **quarters**. Many farmers stack **bales** of hay around their houses to stop cold drafts.

All winter, farmers catch up on sleep and paperwork. Taxes are figured and paid. Stacks of government forms are filled out and mailed. **Seed** is ordered for next year.

But there is still time to celebrate the holidays and be thankful for a good year on the farm.

Opposite page: Winter on the farm.

BC
125309

Glossary

auction (AWK-shun)—a sale where items go to the highest bidder.

bales (BAY-ulz)—round or square bundles of hay.

calving (KAV-ing)—when cows give birth to their babies.

chores (CHORZ)—the jobs that must be done every day on a farm, usually feeding animals and milking cows.

combine (KOM-bine)—a large machine used to harvest grain. Also means the act of harvesting grain with a combine.

cultivator (KULL-tih-vay-ter)—an implement used to uproot and kill weeds.

dairy (DARE-ee)—anything having to do with milk cows.

fertilizer (FIR-tuh-lie-zer)—anything put on the soil to make it richer.

field day—a gathering at a farm to show new systems, seed varieties, or equipment in action.

harvest (HAR-vest)—bringing the crops in from fields and orchards. Harvest can also mean the crops themselves.

insulated (IN-soo-lay-ted)—protected from the cold.

lambing (LAM-ing)—when the ewes (mother lambs) give birth to their babies.

manure (muh-NOOR)—animal waste; it is usually spread on the fields because it is an excellent fertilizer (see fertilizer).

market (MAR-ket)—an open space or covered building where food or cattle are shown for sale.

planter (PLAN-ter)—an implement for mechanically planting seed.

plow—an implement for turning the soil, or the act of turning the soil.

prune (PROON)—cutting excess branches off trees and bushes to develop a healthier and more productive plant.

quarters (KWAR-ters)—a place to live or stay in.

rot—spoil or decay.

seed—new varieties of seed are developed every year, and farmers have to study them to decide what will work best for their soil type and climate. The seed usually comes in 50-pound (23-kg) sacks.

soil (SOY-ull)—part of the Earth's surface in which plants grow; dirt.

spray—a chemical mist applied to crops to kill bugs, fungus, and weeds.

vaccinated (VACK-sih-nay-ted)—giving an animal a shot to prevent disease.

woodlot—a small area of woods on a farm. More common in the east and north.

wormed—giving an animal medicine to kill worms inside of them.

Index

A

animals 16, 24
apples 18
auctions 16
autumn 4

B

barns 14
bugs 12
buildings 14
bushes 6

C

calves 10, 12, 14
cattle 12, 22
cattle shows 16
chores 6, 16
combines 18
corn 10, 14, 18, 22
cotton 10
cows 10
crops 4, 8, 12, 16, 18
cultivator 12

D

dairy 6
deworming 12
dirt 8

E

equipment 16

F

fairs 16
farm equipment shows 16
farm work 4
fences 6
fertilizer 6, 10
field day 16
fields 8, 22
frost 4
fruit growers 6
fruits 16

G

government 24

H

harvest 4, 18, 22, 24
hay 4, 10, 12, 14, 24
holidays 24
horses 12
houses 14, 24

L

lamb 10, 12
leisure 14

M

machinery 6, 10, 22
manure 6
market 22
Midwest 12

O

oxen 8

P

planters 8
plow 4, 8
potatoes 10

R

rain 4, 12
refrigerated trucks 18
rice 10
rodeos 16
roofs 14

S

season 4
seed 6, 10, 24
shed 14
sheep 10, 12, 22
shop 14
soil 6, 8, 18
soybeans 10, 18
spring 4, 6, 8, 10
sugar beets 18
sugar factory 18
summer 4, 12, 14, 16

T

taxes 24
tractors 8
trees 6

V

vaccinate 12
vegetables 10, 16, 18

W

weather 4, 18, 22
weeds 12, 14
West 12
wheat 10, 18
winter 6, 18, 22, 24
woodlots 22